My Book of Animals

Illustrated by Nik Afia

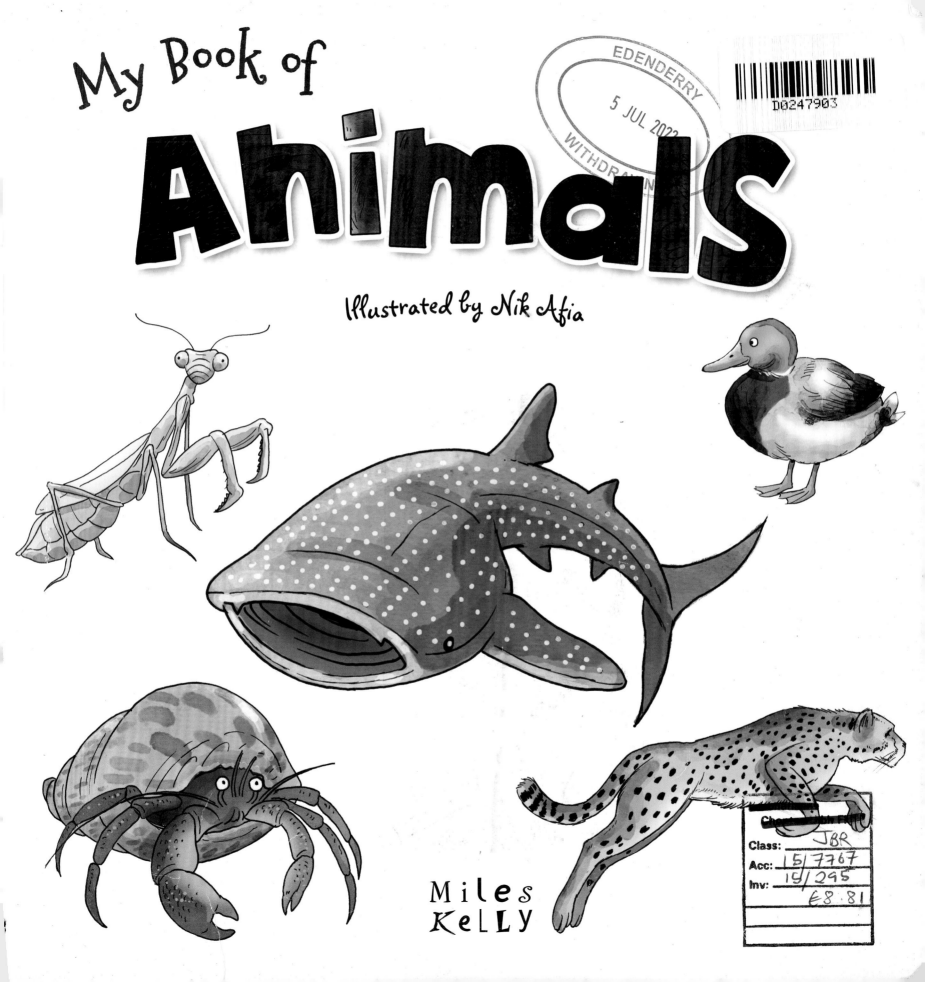

Miles Kelly

Forests and woods

raccoon

Eagles have sharp beaks and claws.

squirrel

wolf

eagle

deer

fox

Which black-and-white animal is eating bamboo?

owl

bear

giant panda

Giant pandas eat bamboo, which is a type of tall grass.

porcupine

badger

mole

bat

Which of these animals can fly?

Rivers and lakes

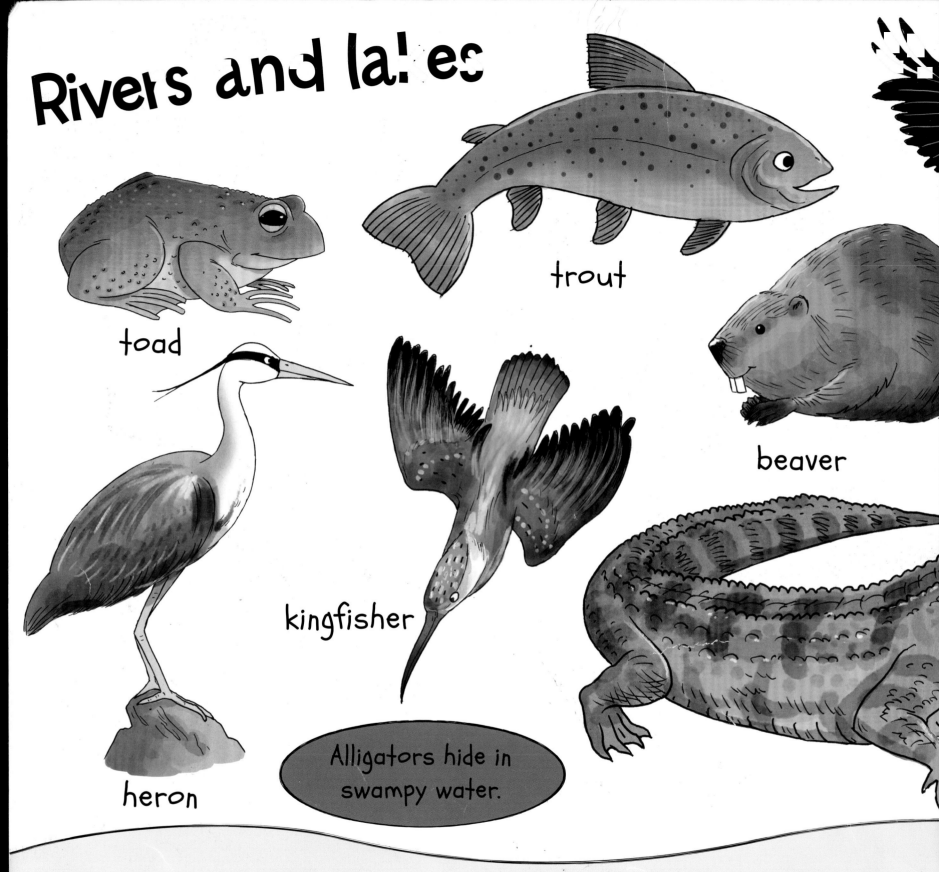

toad

trout

beaver

heron

kingfisher

Alligators hide in swampy water.

Which animal has pink feathers?

pelican

flamingo

otter

Frogs have smooth, damp skin.

alligator

frog

swan

How many of these animals are birds?

In the jungle

All snakes are meat eaters.

toucan

emerald tree boa

butterfly

orang-utan

gorilla

iguana

lemur

What kind of animal is a tarantula?

sloth

tarantula

jaguar

tiger

chameleon

tree frog

monkey

macaw

chimpanzee

tapir

Tigers are the biggest cats.

How many of these animals are cats?

On the seashore

scallop

mussel

gull

Sea anemones catch food with their tentacles.

crab

starfish

sea anemone

Which animal has a body shaped like a star?

oystercatcher

sea urchin

goby

Puffins can carry fish in their beaks.

lobster

puffin

How many of these animals have beaks?

Seas and oceans

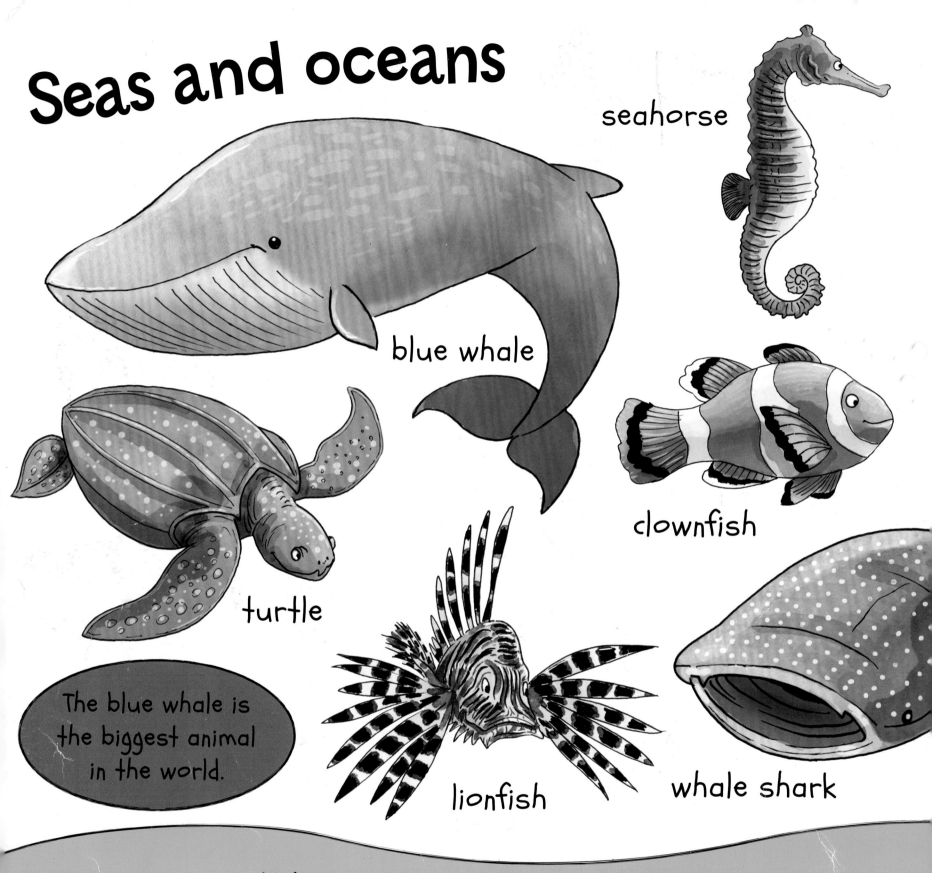

seahorse

blue whale

clownfish

turtle

The blue whale is the biggest animal in the world.

lionfish

whale shark

Which fish looks like a spiky ball?

octopus

dolphin

pufferfish

Pufferfish swallow water to make them swell up.

ray

jellyfish

great white shark

Which of these animals are sharks?

11

In the desert

fennec fox

camel

scorpion

Scorpions can survive without water for months.

lizard

kangaroo rat

sidewinder snake

Which animal has two large humps on its back?

Australian animals

Kangaroos jump using their back legs.

dingo

kangaroo

kookaburra

emu

koala

cassowary

Which bird has a large, horny crest on its head?

African animals

leopard

hyena

vulture

Elephants are the biggest land animals.

elephant

wildebeest

rhinoceros

lion

crocodile

Which animal has a long trunk?

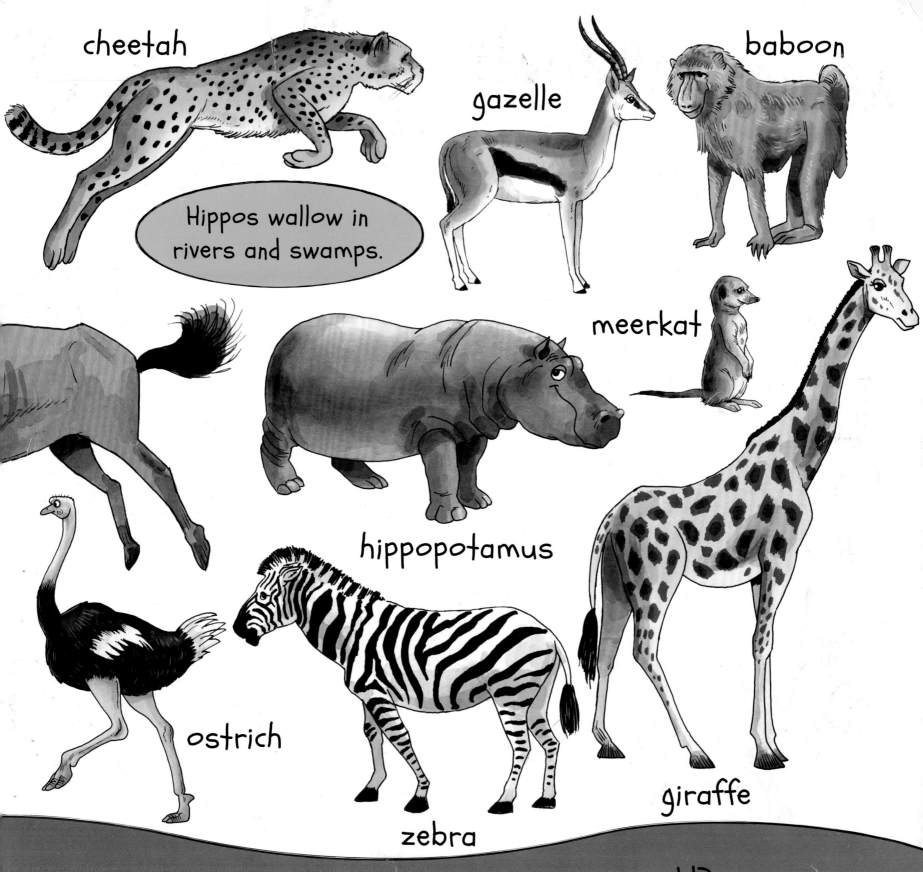

cheetah

gazelle

baboon

Hippos wallow in rivers and swamps.

meerkat

hippopotamus

giraffe

ostrich

zebra

In the Arctic

snowy owl

polar bear

walrus

reindeer

hooded seal

Polar bears are the biggest type of bear.

Arctic fox

narwhal

beluga

Which animal has two large tusks?

In the Antarctic

albatross

leopard seal

southern elephant seal

Orcas are also called killer whales.

emperor penguin

chinstrap penguin

orca

Which penguin is the biggest swimming bird?

On the farm

sheep

goose

pig

Sheep grow thick coats to keep them warm in winter.

cow

chicken

What is the name for a group of cows?

turkey

duck

goat

Ducks use their beaks to clean their feathers.

horse

donkey

Highland bull

How many of these animals have you seen?

Minibeasts

moth

dragonfly

Dragonflies catch food with their legs.

grasshopper

stag beetle

bee

ant

Which minibeast is red with black spots?

spider

caterpillar

centipede

snail

fly

Butterflies are often brightly coloured.

ladybird

praying mantis

butterfly

What does a caterpillar turn into?

Pets

goldfish

pony

guinea pig

Dogs belong to the same family of animals as wolves.

chinchilla

dog

Which of these pets is a reptile?

tortoise

rabbit

gerbil

cat

budgerigar

Budgerigars are also called budgies.

hamster

Can you find?

Look back in your book to see if you can find the following animals.

giant panda

tree frog

crab

octopus

hippopotamus

duck

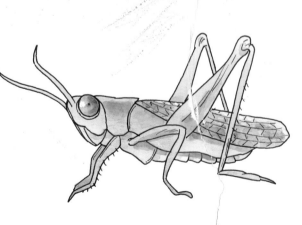

grasshopper

goldfish

24